CW01640750

Boswell Taylor

TEST YOUR CHILD'S General Knowledge

This edition produced exclusively for
WHSMITH

Notes for Parents and Teachers

Each double page consists of a single test. The left-hand page has multi-choice questions with three options for each question. On the right-hand page the questions are open-ended and more difficult. Answers can be written on the dotted lines provided.

On each double page there is also a Time Test to be written on a separate sheet of paper.

The Rating Chart will be found after the Answers at the end of this book. The ratings apply separately to each question section and its Time Test.

You can help to extend your child's General Knowledge.

Encourage your child to ask questions. Answer as fully as you can but never be afraid to acknowledge that you do not know. Follow up with the suggestion that you find out the answer together. Try to build up a small reference library at home. You could begin with an encyclopaedia (one-volumed first, perhaps), a dictionary and the *Guinness Book of Records.*

Encourage your child to use the reference section of the public library. Go with your child if you can, and explore the books together. Some kind of scrap-book can be made at home. Children may like to begin with SPORTS or TOP TWENTY books. They may follow with TOPICAL TIMES full of pictures and items cut from the day's papers and the weekly illustrated magazines.

Don't forget – finding out should be fun!

This edition first published 1982
Second impression 1983
by Hodder and Stoughton Educational,
a division of Hodder and Stoughton Ltd,
Mill Road, Dunton Green, Sevenoaks, Kent

ISBN 0 340 28053 0

Printed and bound in Hong Kong by Colorcraft Ltd.

Phototypeset by Southern Positives and Negatives (SPAN), Lingfield, Surrey

To begin with . . .

Here are three questions, below which are the three possible answers from which you have to choose.

What are the places called where the following animals are kept?

1 pigs..................	2 sheep..................	3 horses..................
a stable	b sty	c fold

Show which answer goes with each question, like this:

1 pigs.......b...........	2 sheep.......c...........	3 horses.......a...........

Now test yourself with these:

What sounds are made by the following animals?

4 turkey..................	5 cow..................	6 pig..................
a grunts	b moos	c gobbles

What name is given to the places used in the following sports?

7 tennis..................	8 boxing..................	9 cricket..................
a ring	b pitch	c court

When a question is asked like this:

1 Which is the largest ocean in the world? ....

write the answer on the dotted line, like this:

1 Which is the largest ocean in the world? .....Pacific.....

Now do these:

2 Whose official home is 10 Downing Street? ....

3 How many strings does a violin have? ....

4 Of which country is the Great Barrier Reef a part? ....

5 What do we call a person who flies an aircraft? ....

Medley 1

What are the sounds made by the following animals?

1 cat..................
a neighs

2 dog..................
b barks

3 horse..................
c purrs

What are the usual contents of the following?

4 kettle..................
a clothes

5 purse..................
b water

6 wardrobe..................
c money

What special names are given to the places where

7 grain is ground?........
a orchard

8 fruit trees grow?........
b mill

9 plays are shown?.......
c theatre

Which fictional characters are linked with the following?

10 'Open Sesame' ....
a Aladdin

11 a glass slipper.........
b Cinderella

12 an old lamp.............
c Ali Baba

Who are the Greek goddesses of the following?

13 hunting..................
a Venus

14 love..................
b Diana

15 wisdom....................
c Athena

In what countries are the following found?

16 the Pyramids..........
a Irish Republic

17 the Blarney Stone ..
b Israel

18 the Wailing Wall......
c Egypt

In which countries are these mountains?

19 Ararat..................
a New Zealand

20 Cotopaxi..................
b Ecuador

21 Cook..................
c Turkey

Of what organizations are the following the headquarters?

22 Scotland Yard.........
a London Police

23 Vatican..................
b US Defence

24 Pentagon ....
c Roman Catholic Church

What are measured by the following?

25 the cran..................
a fish

26 knots..................
b height of horse

27 hands..................
c a ship's speed

What single words can be used for the following?

28 so let it be...............
a eureka

29 higher still ....
b amen

30 'I have found it!' ......
c excelsior

31 According to the rhyme what kind of meat did Jack Sprat eat? ....

32 What do we call the yellow part of an egg? ....

33 What was the ship on which Nelson died? ....

34 Sour milk consists of curds and what else? ....

35 Where is the rattlesnake's rattle? ....

36 What tree gives us the acorn? ....

37 What relation to you is your mother's father? ....

38 Whose knights sat at the Round Table? ....

39 What flower is the national emblem of England? ....

40 By what name are the Yeoman of the Guard at the Tower of London better known? ....

41 How many sides has an octagon? ....

42 Where in your body is your 'funny bone'? ....

43 How many dwarfs helped Snow White? ....

44 How many playing cards are there in an ordinary pack? ....

45 How many men did a Roman centurion command? ....

Time Test

How many can you write down in the given time?
On a separate sheet of paper make three columns:

Fish	Girls' Names	Islands

Write the names you know. Have your list checked.

Count 2 for each correct answer. Check your rating.

Time allowed: 7 and 8 year olds – 3 minutes
9 and 10 year olds – 2 minutes
11 year olds and over – 1 minute

People

Who would be likely to use the following?

1 plough..................	2 saw..................	3 telescope..................
a astronomer	b farmer	c carpenter

What do we call the chief persons connected with the following?

4 army..................	5 newspaper................	6 ship..................
a editor	b captain	c general

Who worships in this kind of building?

7 synagogue................	8 mosque..................	9 church..................
a Christian	b Muslim	c Jew

What do we call the persons who sell the following?

10 vegetables..............	11 cigarettes................	12 tools..................
a greengrocer	b ironmonger	c tobacconist

What animals are associated with the following?

13 Father Christmas....	14 Dick Whittington....	15 Dick Turpin ....
a cat	b horse	c reindeer

Who are the patron saints of these countries?

16 Scotland..................	17 Ireland..................	18 Wales..................
a St David	b St Patrick	c St Andrew

What important people live at these residences?

19 Windsor Castle	20 The Vatican............	21 The White House.....
a The Pope	b British sovereign	c US president

What special feat made these people 'famous firsts'?

22 Edmund Hillary.......	23 Neil Armstrong	24 Yuri Gagarin ....
a travelled in space	b climbed Everest	c landed on the Moon

With what inventions are these persons associated?

25 Alexander G. Bell ...	26 James Watt............	27 Wright brothers........
a steam engine	b telephone	c aeroplane

Who founded these organizations?

28 Salvation Army.......	29 Scouts.....................	30 Red Cross................
a Jean H. Dunant	b William Booth	c Lord Baden-Powell

31 Of what country was Cleopatra queen? ....

32 Who was the apostle who betrayed Jesus? ....

33 Who founded the Muslim faith? ....

34 Who first brought tobacco to Britain? ....

35 What title was given to the German Emperors? ....

36 Which president of the United States was a film actor? ....

37 Who was the president of the United States at the time of the 'Watergate Affair'? ....

38 Who was the Russian who wrote *War and Peace*? ....

39 Who was the first woman to fly in space? ....

40 Who was the Brazilian said to be the world's greatest soccer player in the 1970s? ....

41 Which surgeon made the first heart transplant? ....

42 What country does the pop group ABBA come from? ....

43 Who was the first woman prime minister of Britain? ....

44 Who was the father of Queen Elizabeth II? ....

45 Which national leader was famous for his 'Book of Thoughts'? ....

Time Test

How many can you write down in the given time?
On a separate sheet of paper make three columns:

Footballers   Painters   Inventors

Write the names you know. Have your list checked.

Count 2 for each correct answer. Check your rating.

Time allowed: 7 and 8 year olds – 3 minutes
9 and 10 year olds – 2 minutes
11 year olds – 1 minute

Food and Drink

What foods do we associate with the following?

1 Shrove Tuesday........ 2 Good Friday............. 3 Christmas Day..........

a mince pies b pancakes c hot cross buns

Which animals supply the following?

4 mutton.................. 5 pork.................. 6 beef..................

a pigs b bullocks c sheep

What kinds of food and drink have these place names?

7 Brussels.................. 8 Burgundy.................. 9 Stilton..................

a vegetable b cheese c wine

What is the main ingredient of these foods?

10 toad-in-the-hole........... 11 Welsh rarebit.......... 12 angels-on-horseback...........

a sardines b sausage c cheese

For which food are the following countries noted?

13 Turkey.................. 14 France.................. 15 Italy..................

a pizza b kebab c snails

From which countries do these cheeses come?

16 Edam.................. 17 Gorgonzola............ 18 Brie..................

a Holland b Italy c France

To which fruits do the following names refer?

19 Jaffa.................. 20 Conference........... 21 Victoria..................

a plum b pear c orange

Which of these vegetables grow in the following ways?

22 under the ground.... 23 on the ground......... 24 on stems..................

a broad beans b carrot c marrow

What drinks are made from the following?

25 malt and hops......... 26 apples.................. 27 molasses..................

a cider b rum c beer

What kind of foods are the following?

28 cutlet.................. 29 ketchup.................. 30 cheddar..................

a meat b cheese c sauce

31 What is grown in fields called paddies? ....

32 Are anchovies vegetables or fish? ....

33 What fish may become a kipper or a bloater? ....

34 What sauce is usually served with lamb? ....

35 What kind of pastry is used in making éclairs? ....

36 What do the seeds of the cacao tree make? ....

37 What fruit is generally used to make marmalade? ....

38 What is porridge usually made from? ....

39 What kind of meat provides sirloin? ....

40 What is the insect that gives us honey? ....

41 What beverage comes from China, Ceylon and India? ....

42 What is butter produced from? ....

43 What kind of tree or bush supplies blackberries? ....

44 What is yoghurt made from? ....

45 What part of the plant is used to make mustard? ....

Time Test

How many can you write down in the given time?
On a separate sheet of paper make three columns:

Drinks	Favourite Foods	Fruits

Write the names you know. Have your list checked.

Count 2 for each correct answer. Check your rating.

Time allowed: 7 and 8 year olds – 3 minutes
9 and 10 year olds – 2 minutes
11 year olds – 1 minute

Medley 2

In nursery rhymes what numbers apply to the following?

1 miles to Babylon.......	2 bags of wool............	3 Duke of York's men...
a 3	b 70	c 10,000

What names are given to the young of the following?

4 hare..................	5 swan..................	6 deer..................
a fawn	b leveret	c cygnet

What name is given to the people at the following?

7 concert..................	8 church service..........	9 art gallery ....
a viewers	b audience	c congregation

What kind of animals in stories are the following?

10 Tarka..................	11 Eeyore..................	12 Captain Flint...........
a donkey	b parrot	c otter

Where are the following important places?

13 Red Square............	14 Forbidden City..........	15 St Peter's Square.....
a Moscow (USSR)	b Rome (Italy)	c Peking (China)

Which Biblical people were known for the following?

16 strength..................	17 patience..................	18 wisdom..................
a Solomon	b Samson	c Job

Who wrote about the following naughty girls?

19 Ramona the Pest....	20 St Trinian's.............	21 Pippi Longstocking....
a Astrid Lindgren	b Beverley Cleary	c Ronald Searle

Where are the following found?

22 pampas..................	23 tundra..................	24 the Rand..................
a South Africa	b North Russia	c South America

Which creatures in myths had the following unusual features?

25 two faces................	26 three mouths..........	27 one eye ....
a the Cyclops	b Janus	c Cerberus

What did each of the following devise?

28 Isaac Pitman..........	29 Admiral Beaufort....	30 John Curwen..........
a wind force scale	b tonic sol-fa	c shorthand

31 Of what word is 'fridge' the shortened form? ....

32 Which is the longest river in the world? ....

33 Who was the leader of the 'Merry Men' of Sherwood Forest? ....

34 How many years are there in a decade? ....

35 In the nursery rhyme, what did Little Tommy Green do? ....

36 In English cricket how many balls are bowled in a normal over? ....

37 What is the rope that a cowboy uses called? ....

38 What kind of book did Mrs Beeton write? ....

39 What colour is the cornflower? ....

40 What colour are babies' eyes at birth? ....

41 What woman's name is linked with waxworks? ....

42 What is the colour of a sapphire? ....

43 What is a puffin? ....

44 Where does lava come from? ....

45 What country has the word 'Suomi' on its stamps? ....

Time Test

How many can you write down in the given time?
On a separate sheet of paper make three columns:

Clothes	Countries	Tools

Write the names you know. Have your list checked.

Count 2 for each correct answer. Check your rating.

Time allowed: 7 and 8 year olds – 3 minutes
9 and 10 year olds – 2 minutes
11 year olds – 1 minute

Science and Machines

What do the following measure?

1 metre..................	2 second..................	3 litre..................
a liquid	b length	c time

Where are these instruments likely to be found?

4 telescope	5 speedometer.............	6 metronome ....
a in a music room	b in an observatory	c in a motor car

Who would be the most likely users of these tools?

7 hoe..................	8 chisel..................	9 razor..................
a gardener	b barber	c carpenter

What are studied in these subjects?

10 geology..................	11 zoology..................	12 botany..................
a animals	b flowers	c rocks

What do you associate these substances with?

13 fluorine..................	14 yeast..................	15 mercury..................
a bread	b toothpaste	c thermometers

Which of the planets are the following?

16 the largest	17 nearest to Earth	18 the smallest.............
a Jupiter	b Venus	c Mercury

What elements are used in the following?

19 wire..................	20 coins..................	21 lamps..................
a neon	b copper	c nickel

Who invented the following?

22 ball-point pen	23 bicycle tyre.............	24 safety-razor.............
a Dunlop	b Biro	c Gillette

In which part of your body are the following?

25 ribs..................	26 skull..................	27 shin..................
a head	b chest	c leg

Who discovered the following?

28 vaccination	29 penicillin.................	30 radium ....
a Alexander Fleming	b the Curies	c Dr Edward Jenner

31 What is coal made of? ....

32 At what temperature on the Centigrade thermometer does water boil? ....

33 At what temperature on the Centigrade thermometer does water turn to ice? ....

34 What is the machine that takes photographs called? ....

35 What does a sundial measure? ....

36 What is the name given to a ship which travels under water? ....

37 What is the machine called that measures gas or electricity used? ....

38 What instrument magnifies tiny objects? ....

39 What machine is used in offices for letter-writing? ....

40 What instrument held in the hand gives directions? ....

41 What instrument tells if surfaces are level? ....

42 What machine takes photographs through the body? ....

43 What instrument is used for drawing straight lines? ....

44 What device will attract iron nails and filings? ....

45 What device tracks aircraft in the sky? ....

Time Test

How many can you write down in the given time?
On a separate sheet of paper make three columns:

Machines	Instruments	Metals

Write the names you know. Have your list checked.

Count 2 for each correct answer. Check your rating.

Time allowed: 7 and 8 year olds – 3 minutes
9 and 10 year olds – 2 minutes
11 year olds – 1 minute

History

What king or queen is connected with the following?

1 Domesday Book	2 Spanish Armada.......	3 Magna Carta ....
a William the Conqueror	b Queen Elizabeth	c King John

Which kings were known by these nicknames?

4 The Unready............	5 Coeur-de-Lion.........	6 The Great...................
a Ethelred	b Alfred	c Richard I

Who was the leader of the following?

7 The Red Shirts	8 The Lollards	9 The Nazis...................
a Hitler	b Garibaldi	c Wycliffe

Who won these victories?

10 Blenheim..................	11 Agincourt	12 Borodino..................
a Duke of Marlborough	b King Henry V	c Napoleon

In which years did these Civil Wars begin?

13 American..................	14 Spanish..................	15 English..................
a 1642	b 1936	c 1861

In which war were these battles fought?

16 Balaclava...............	17 Bosworth Field	18 Poitiers ....
a Wars of the Roses	b Hundred Years' War	c Crimean War

Who founded the following?

19 The Post Office.......	20 The Methodists.......	21 London Police ....
a John Wesley	b Sir Robert Peel	c Sir Rowland Hill

With what king or queen are these people associated?

22 Thomas Cromwell..	23 William Cecil..........	24 Benjamin Disraeli...
a Queen Elizabeth I	b Queen Victoria	c King Henry VIII

With which revolutions are these persons associated?

25 Lenin....................	26 William of Orange..	27 Robespierre.............
a 'Glorious Revolution'	b French Revolution	c Russian Revolution

Of which country were these persons active patriots?

28 Churchill.................	29 Bismarck................	30 Joan of Arc ....
a Germany	b England	c France

31 Where was Napoleon Bonaparte born? ....

32 Who was the British queen who resisted the Romans? ....

33 Where was Alexander the Great born? ....

34 Which English queen was called 'Good'? ....

35 What nickname was given to Cromwell's troops? ....

36 Who was called the 'Fuhrer' in the 1930s? ....

37 Who was murdered in Canterbury Abbey? ....

38 What was France called when it was part of the Roman Empire? ....

39 Who was the Roman general who landed in Britain in 55 and 54 B.C.? ....

40 Who was president during the American Civil War? ....

41 The Lancastrians wore red roses. Who wore white? ....

42 What great city fell to the Turks in 1453? ....

43 Which British monarch lived longest? ....

44 Where are the headquarters of the United Nations? ....

45 Whose landing at Sydney in 1788 is remembered on Australia Day? ....

Time Test

How many can you write down in the given time?
On a separate sheet of paper make three columns:

Castles | Cathedrals | Kings and Queens

Write the names you know. Have your list checked.

Count 2 for each correct answer. Check your rating.

Time allowed: 7 and 8 year olds – 3 minutes
9 and 10 year olds – 2 minutes
11 year olds – 1 minute

Medley 3

What sounds are made by the following?

1 little bells	2 car brakes	3 clock ....
a tick	b tinkle	c screech

What are the special names given to places where the following are made?

4 beer	5 bread	6 coins ....
a mint	b bakery	c brewery

What are the names of the places where the following are sold?

7 meat	8 milk	9 flowers ....
a dairy	b butchers	c florists

Who were the wives of these famous men?

10 Robin Hood	11 King Arthur	12 Othello ....
a Guinevere	b Maid Marian	c Desdemona

What countries are associated with the following?

13 springbok	14 kangaroo	15 kiwi ....
a South Africa	b New Zealand	c Australia

What are known by the following Australian names?

16 dingo	17 corroboree	18 didgeridoo ....
a social party	b wild dog	c musical instrument

Which nationalities are given these nicknames?

19 Uncle Sam	20 John Bull	21 Paddy ....
a English	b Irish	c American

In heraldry what colours correspond to the following?

22 green	23 red	24 black ....
a sable	b vert	c gules

What kind of articles are associated with the following?

25 Stradivarius	26 Chippendale	27 Constable ....
a furniture	b picture	c violin

Where are these famous art galleries?

28 Louvre	29 Tate	30 Hermitage ....
a Leningrad, Russia	b Paris, France	c London, England

31 What is the name of the first month in the calendar year? ....

32 What is the city with the largest population? ....

33 Of what word is 'gym' a shortened form? ....

34 Where was Jesus Christ born? ....

35 Where was Mohammed born? ....

36 What battle was fought at Battle? ....

37 What do silkworms normally feed on? ....

38 What detective was created by Conan Doyle? ....

39 Where are cows respected as sacred animals? ....

40 What did the Romans call London? ....

41 What is the main ingredient used to make an omelette? ....

42 What country's flag shows a hammer and a sickle? ....

43 What is the colour of a Jersey cow? ....

44 What was the name of King Arthur's sword? ....

45 In Parliament what does a successful bill become? ....

Time Test

How many can you write down in the given time?
On a separate sheet of paper make three columns:

Continents   Breeds of Dog   Musical Instruments

Write the names you know. Have your list checked.

Count 2 for each correct answer. Check your rating.

Time allowed: 7 and 8 year olds – 3 minutes
9 and 10 year olds – 2 minutes
11 year olds – 1 minute

Books and Words

In what kind of book will you find information about the following?

1 telephone numbers...	2 maps..................	3 words..................
a dictionary	b atlas	c directory

What kind of creatures are these animals in stories?

4 Macavity..................	5 Black Beauty	6 Mrs Tiggy-Winkle......
a cat	b hedgehog	c horse

In which books can these villains be found?

7 Long John Silver......	8 Captain Hook	9 Fagin..................
a *Oliver Twist*	b *Peter Pan*	c *Treasure Island*

In which novels are these heroines to be found?

10 Arrietty..................	11 Little Nell................	12 Jo............................
a *Little Women*	b *Old Curiosity Shop*	c *The Borrowers*

What are these remarkable characters?

13 Stig of the Dump....	14 The Psammead.......	15 Mrs Frisby ....
a fieldmouse	b sand-fairy	c caveman

What kind of books are the following?

16 *White Fang*.............	17 *Eagle of the Ninth*..	18 *Trillions*....................
a science-fiction	b animal story	c historical story

Who wrote about these characters?

19 Mole and Toad.......	20 Gulliver....................	21 Mowgli..................
a Rudyard Kipling	b Jonathan Swift	c Kenneth Grahame

In which country are these stories set?

22 *Little Women*	23 *Prester John*...........	24 *Heidi*..................
a Switzerland	b Africa	c USA

What kind of works were written or told by the following?

25 Aesop..................	26 Shakespeare	27 Homer..................
a plays	b myths	c fables

Which writers set their books in the following places?

27 Lake District...........	29 Moominvalley.........	30 Wisconsin (USA)....
a Laura Ingalls Wilder	b Arthur Ransome	c Tove Jansson

31 What are the five vowels? ....

32 What kind of stories did Hans Andersen write? ....

33 Who went to sea in a 'beautiful pea-green boat'? ....

34 At the Mad Hatter's tea-party who ended up in a pot of tea? ....

35 How many fiddlers did King Cole have? ....

36 What pest did the Pied Piper get rid of? ....

37 In a book by Charles Dickens, who asked for more? ....

38 In *Peter Pan*, what was Captain Hook afraid of? ....

39 In Greek mythology, who was king of the gods? ....

40 How many lines are there in a limerick? ....

41 In *Pilgrim's Progress*, what was the name of the pilgrim? ....

42 Who travelled to Lilliput? ....

43 In the story by Roald Dahl, what kind of factory does Charlie Bucket get from Mr Wonka? ....

44 What is the nationality of Asterix, the cartoon character invented by Goscinny? ....

45 Who wrote about Professor Branestawm? ....

Time Test

How many can you write down in the given time?
On a separate sheet of paper make three columns:

Book Titles   Authors   Story Characters

Write the names you know. Have your list checked.

Count 2 for each correct answer. Check your rating.

Time allowed: 7 and 8 year olds – 3 minutes
9 and 10 year olds – 2 minutes
11 year olds – 1 minute

Sports and Games

Which countries do these famous soccer teams come from?

1 Juventus.................. 2 Ajax.................. 3 Real Madrid..............

a Netherlands b Italy c Spain

With which game or sport are the following associated?

4 Wimbledon................ 5 Lords.................. 6 Le Mans ....

a motor racing b cricket c lawn tennis

In what games are these terms used?

7 castling...................... 8 huffing .... 9 double twenty............

a darts b chess c draughts

In which sports are these terms used?

10 innings.................. 11 love.................. 12 relay..................

a athletics b cricket c tennis

Which country won the World Cup for soccer in the following years?

13 1966.................. 14 1974.................. 15 1978..................

a West Germany b Argentina c England

In which sports are these trophies awarded?

16 Davis Cup .... 17 Calcutta Cup .... 18 Ryder Cup.................

a golf b rugby football c lawn tennis

With what sports or recreations are these clubs connected?

19 Harlem Globe-Trotters .... 20 Royal and Ancient .... 21 Harlequins................

a rugby football b basket-ball c golf

In which sports have these persons gained their fame?

22 Mohammed Ali....... 23 Jackie Stewart .... 24 Robin Cousins..........

a boxing b ice skating c motor racing

How many persons comprise a team in these sports?

25 field hockey............ 26 netball.................. 27 polo...........................

a 7 b 11 c 4

In what countries are these the principal national games?

28 baseball.................. 29 ice hockey .... 30 hurling ....

a Irish Republic b United States c Canada

31 In what sport might you do a crawl and win? ....

32 How many pieces are there in a game of draughts? ....

33 What game is played on links with clubs? ....

34 In what sport is the 'Yellow Jersey' worn? ....

35 Who plays for the Ashes? ....

36 How many miles are run in the Olympic Marathon? ....

37 In lawn tennis what is an ace? ....

38 How many points does a 'bull' in darts score? ....

39 Who first ran a mile in less than 4 minutes? ....

40 On which river is the famous University Boat Race contested? ....

41 What sport is sometimes described as 'All-In'? ....

42 What is the maximum number of sets in a major men's tennis match? ....

43 In soccer what does a team get if they are awarded a penalty? ....

44 In which sport are Lonsdale belts awarded? ....

45 In a boat race what does the coxswain do? ....

Time Test

How many can you write down in the given time?
On a separate sheet of paper make three columns:

Sports Day Events	Outdoor Sports played with a ball	Indoor Games played on a board

Write the names you know. Have your list checked.

Count 2 for each correct answer. Check your rating.

Time allowed: 7 and 8 year olds – 3 minutes
9 and 10 year olds – 2 minutes
11 year olds – 1 minute

Medley 4

What sounds are made by the following?

1 donkey..................	2 wolf..................	3 pigeon..................
a howls	b coos	c brays

What are the fresh fruits that produce the following?

4 raisins..................	5 prunes..................	6 coconuts..................
a plums	b copra	c grapes

What are the special names given to the following places?

7 burial places.............	8 water stores..............	9 car stores....................
a reservoirs	b cemetaries	c garages

What colours are the following shades?

10 ultramarine.............	11 emerald...................	12 scarlet ....
a green	b red	c blue

How many edges and sides have the following?

13 a cone..................	14 a cylinder................	15 a cube..................
a 2 edges 3 sides	b 1 edge 2 sides	c 8 edges 6 sides

With which countries are the following people associated?

16 geishas....................	17 mounties.................	18 gurkhas ....
a Nepal	b Canada	c Japan

With which real characters are the following associated?

19 an oak tree	20 an apple	21 a spider....................
a King Charles II	b Sir Isaac Newton	c Robert the Bruce

What are the main territorial divisions of the following countries?

22 Switzerland............	23 France..................	24 Canada..................
a departments	b provinces	c cantons

With what would you be concerned if you were a member of the following?

25 WHO..................	26 IMF..................	27 UNICEF...................
a children	b finance	c health

What are the simple names of the following pastimes?

28 numismatics...........	29 pyrotechnics	30 philately ....
a stamp collecting	b coin collecting	c firework displays

31 What colour mixed with blue makes green? ....

32 What does the 'X' in Roman figures stand for? ....

33 What is the chief export of Zambia? ....

34 What name is given to the Friday before Easter Day? ....

35 How many Georges have reigned in Britain altogether? ....

36 Which month is sometimes called the 'Merry Month'? ....

37 What animal may suffer from distemper and rabies? ....

38 In the fairy tale what did the 'Ugly Duckling' grow into? ....

39 Where is the famous leaning tower? ....

40 What is the Russian 'sputnik'? ....

41 Who was the first president of Tanzania? ....

42 What is the name given to the month of fasting in the Muslim year? ....

43 What is the chief money unit in Canada? ....

44 What mountain range separates Spain and France? ....

45 How often do the Olympic Games take place? ....

Time Test

How many can you write down in the given time?
On a separate sheet of paper make three columns:

Boys' Names | Occupations | Vegetables

Write the names you know. Have your list checked.

Count 2 for each correct answer. Check your rating.

Time allowed: 7 and 8 year olds – 3 minutes
9 and 10 year olds – 2 minutes
11 year olds – 1 minute

Travel

In which countries are these tourist attractions?

1 Pyramids.................. 2 Colosseum.............. 3 Parthenon..................
a Greece b Egypt c Italy

Which form of transport is associated wth the following?

4 Wright brothers......... 5 Stephenson................ 6 Gottlieb Daimler ....
a motor car b railway train c aeroplane

Which great men sailed in these ships?

7 Santa Maria............. 8 Endeavour................. 9 Golden Hind..............
a Sir Francis Drake b Christopher Columbus c Captain James Cook

In which countries are important roads named the following?

10 freeways................. 11 autostrada .... 12 autobahnen ....
a USA b Italy c Germany

What kind of vehicle had this famous name?

13 The Rocket............. 14 Cutty Sark .... 15 Nautilus...................
a clipper ship b submarine c locomotive

Who were the famous travellers in these ships?

16 Argo.................. 17 Beagle.................. 18 Mayflower...............
a Jason b Pilgrim Fathers c Charles Darwin

Which cities are near these?

19 Table Mountain...... 20 Mount Cook........... 21 Mount Fujiyama......
a Tokyo b Cape Town c Christchurch

In which towns are these railway stations?

22 Gard du Nord.......... 23 Grand Central......... 24 Euston ....
a London b New York c Paris

Which cities are served by the following airports?

25 Leonardo da Vinci.. 26 Schipol .... 27 Orly ....
a Paris b Rome c Amsterdam

Which are the foreign ports that stand near the mouths of these rivers?

28 Seine.................. 29 Hudson.................. 30 St Lawrence............
a Montreal b Le Havre c New York

31 What is the fuel normally used by motor cars? ....

32 What was the fuel used for the first railway locomotives? ....

33 What was the name of the first jet airliner in regular service? ....

34 What is the *Concorde*? ....

35 What are railway sleepers? ....

36 Why do ports have dry docks? ....

37 What country is sometimes called 'The Holy Land'? ....

38 Where is the Sea of Tranquillity? ....

39 What is the shortest sea crossing between England and France? ..../.............

40 What countries are connected by the Simplon Tunnel? ..../.............

41 Where did Lord Nuffield build his Morris works? ....

42 Of what word is 'bus' a shortened form? ....

43 How long is the Panama Canal: 50 or 500 or 5,000 miles? ....

44 What colour flag means infectious sickness on board ship? ....

45 Which country operates the Qantas airline? ....

Time Test

How many can you write down in the given time?
On a separate sheet of paper make three columns:

Makes of Motor Car | Kinds of Ship | Names of Airlines

Write the names you know. Have your list checked.

Count 2 for each correct answer. Check your rating.

Time allowed: 7 and 8 year olds – 3 minutes
9 and 10 year olds – 2 minutes
11 year olds – 1 minute

Geography

In which country are these cities?

1 Glasgow..................	2 Manchester	3 Melbourne.................
a England	b Australia	c Scotland

Of which country are these the capital cities?

4 Paris..................	5 Madrid..................	6 Delhi..................
a Spain	b France	c India

In which continent are these ranges of mountains?

7 Andes..................	8 Atlas..................	9 Alps..................
a Europe	b South America	c Africa

In which mountain range are these peaks?

10 Mount Everest	11 Matterhorn.............	12 Mount Logan ....
a Rocky Mountains	b Himalayas	c Alps

On which river do these towns stand?

13 Dublin..................	14 Vienna..................	15 Cologne..................
a Danube	b Rhine	c Liffey

What are the national emblems of these countries?

16 Ireland	17 Scotland.................	18 Wales..................
a leek	b thistle	c shamrock

In which country do or did these people live?

19 Bretons..................	20 Maori..................	21 Bedouins.................
a Arabia	b Brittany, France	c New Zealand

In which countries are these money units used?

22 lira..................	23 rouble..................	24 rupee..................
a Italy	b India	c Russia

In what group of islands will these islands be found?

25 Jersey	26 Jamaica	27 Majorca...................
a Caribbean	b Balearic	c Channel

In what cities are these special places to be found?

28 Kremlin..................	29 Vatican..................	30 Eiffel Tower.............
a Rome (Italy)	b Moscow (USSR)	c Paris (France)

31 What is the highest mountain in the world? ....

32 Which country produces the most coffee? ....

33 Into which ocean does the river Amazon flow? ....

34 In which country is Mount Popocatepetl? ....

35 How did the Dead Sea get its name? ....

36 What country is known as the 'Emerald Isle'? ....

37 What country has two main islands, one called North and the other called South? ....

38 On which river is the Aswan High Dam? ....

39 What is the sacred river of the Hindus? ....

40 Which Australian state has the largest population? ....

41 On which island do Manx people live? ....

42 What is the largest island in the world? ....

43 What is the largest of Japan's many islands? ....

44 What is the Sahara? ....

45 In Australia is 'Alice Springs' a river, town or mountain? ....

Time Test

How many can you write down in the given time?
On a separate sheet of paper make three columns:

Towns	Countries	Rivers

Write the names you know. Have your list checked.

Count 2 for each correct answer. Check your rating.

Time allowed: 7 and 8 year olds – 3 minutes
9 and 10 year olds – 2 minutes
11 year olds – 1 minute

Nature

How many legs do these creatures have?

1 spider.................. 2 fly.................. 3 tiger..................

a four b eight c six

Name the parent of these young creatures

4 chicken.................. 5 puppy.................. 6 kitten..................

a hen b dog c cat

Give the name of the young of these creatures

7 horse.................. 8 sheep.................. 9 goat..................

a kid b foal c lamb

What name is given to the home of these animals?

10 dog.................. 11 rabbit.................. 12 horse..................

a stable b hutch c kennel

What do we call a group of the following?

13 cattle.................. 14 sheep.................. 15 puppies..................

a litter b flock c herd

Give the name of the young of these creatures

16 cow.................. 17 leopard.................. 18 salmon..................

a cub b calf c parr

What name is given to the home of these creatures?

19 badger.................. 20 hare.................. 21 fox..................

a sett b earth c form

What do we call a group of the following?

22 lions.................. 23 wolves.................. 24 whales..................

a pack b school c pride

What do we call the females of these males?

25 boar.................. 26 buck.................. 27 gander..................

a sow b goose c doe

What things in nature suffer from these pests or diseases?

28 foot and mouth....... 29 Colorado beetle...... 30 swine fever..............

a pigs b potatoes c cattle

31 Where does the kangaroo carry its young? ....

32 What small creature spins a web to catch its prey? ....

33 In what part of its body does the camel store its fat? ....

34 What large animal uses a trunk to drink water? ....

35 What is the bird with a familiar call that does not build a nest? ....

36 What is the animal with the longest neck? ....

37 What is the largest bird in the world? ....

38 What member of the cat family is the fastest animal over short distances? ....

39 What is the New Zealand bird that has become the country's emblem? ....

40 What is the smallest bird in the world? ....

41 What flower has a name which means 'lion's tooth'? ....

42 Which insect with the same name as a game, sings and lives near fires? ....

43 What name is given to a fox's tail? ....

44 What bird has a call 'too-whit, too-whoo', and is heard at night? ....

45 What animal is proverbial for changing its colour? ....

Time Test

How many can you write down in the given time?
On a separate sheet of paper make three columns:

Animals	Birds	Flowers and Trees

Write the names you know. Have your list checked.

Count 2 for each correct answer. Check your rating.

Time allowed: 7 and 8 year olds – 3 minutes
9 and 10 year olds – 2 minutes
11 year olds – 1 minute

Answers

Medley 1

1c, 2b, 3a: 4b, 5c, 6a: 7b, 8a, 9c: 10c, 11b, 12a: 13b, 14a, 15c:
16c, 17a, 18b: 19c, 20b, 21a: 22a, 23c, 24b: 25a, 26c, 27b: 28b, 29c, 30a
31. lean 32. yolk 33. H.M.S. Victory 34. whey 35. in the tail 36. oak
37. grandfather 38. King Arthur's 39. rose 40. Beefeaters 41. 8
42. elbow 43. 7 44. 52+2 jokers 45. 100

People

1b, 2c, 3a: 4c, 5a, 6b: 7c, 8b, 9a: 10a, 11c, 12b: 13c, 14a, 15b:
16c, 17b, 18a: 19b, 20a, 21c: 22b, 23c, 24a: 25b, 26a, 27c: 28b, 29c, 30a
31. Egypt 32. Judas 33. Mohammed 34. Sir Walter Raleigh 35. Kaiser
36. Ronald Reagan 37. Richard Nixon 38. Leo Tolstoy
39. Valentina Tereshkova 40. Pelé 41. Christiaan Barnard 42. Sweden
43. Margaret Thatcher 44. King George VI 45. Chairman Mao Tse-tung

Food and Drink

1b, 2c, 3a: 4c, 5a, 6b: 7a, 8c, 9b: 10b, 11c, 12a: 13b, 14c, 15a:
16a, 17b, 18a: 19c, 20b, 21a: 22b, 23c, 24a: 25c, 26a, 27b: 28a, 29c, 30b
31. rice 32. fish 33. herring 34. mint 35. choux pastry
36. cocoa/chocolate 37. oranges 38. oatmeal 39. beef 40. bee
41. tea 42. milk 43. bramble 44. milk 45. seeds

Medley 2

1b, 2a, 3c: 4b, 5c, 6a: 7b, 8c, 9a: 10c, 11a, 12b: 13a, 14c, 15b:
16b, 17c, 18a: 19b, 20c, 21a: 22c, 23b, 24a: 25b, 26c, 27a: 28c, 29a, 30b
31. refrigerator 32. Nile 33. Robin Hood 34. 10 35. put Pussy in the well 36. 6 37. lariat/lasso 38. cookery 39. blue 40. blue
41. Madame Tussaud 42. blue 43. sea-bird 44. volcanoes 45. Finland

Science and Machines

1b, 2c, 3a: 4b, 5c, 6a: 7a, 8c, 9b: 10c, 11a, 12b: 13b, 14a, 15c:
16a, 17b, 18c: 19b, 20c, 21a: 22b, 23a, 24c: 25b, 26a, 27c: 28c, 29a, 30b
31. carbon 32. 100° 33. 0° 34. camera 35. time 36. submarine
37. meter 38. microscope 39. typewriter 40. compass 41. spirit-level
42. X-rays 43. ruler 44. magnet 45. radar

History

1a, 2b, 3c: 4a, 5c, 6b: 7b, 8c, 9a: 10a, 11b, 12c: 13c, 14b, 15a:
16c, 17a, 18b: 19c, 20a, 21b: 22c, 23a, 24b: 25c, 26a, 27b: 28b, 29a, 30c
31. Corsica 32. Boadicea 33. Macedonia, Greece 34. Elizabeth I (Bess)
35. Ironsides 36. Adolf Hitler 37. Thomas à Becket 38. Gaul
39. Julius Caesar 40. Abraham Lincoln 41. Yorkists 42. Constantinople
43. Queen Victoria 44. New York 45. Captain Phillip

Medley 3

1b, 2c, 3a: 4c, 5b, 6a: 7b, 8a, 9c: 10b, 11a, 12c: 13a, 14c, 15b:
16b, 17a, 18c: 19c, 20a, 21b: 22b, 23c, 24a: 25c, 26a, 27b: 28b, 29c, 30a
31. January 32. Shanghai, China 33. gymnasium 34. Bethlehem
35. Mecca 36. Hastings 37. mulberry leaves 38. Sherlock Holmes
39. India 40. Londinium 41. egg 42. Russia (USSR) 43. light brown
44. Excalibur 45. act/law

Books and Words

1c, 2b, 3a: 4a, 5c, 6b: 7c, 8b, 9a: 10c, 11b, 12a: 13c, 14b, 15a:
16b, 17c, 18a: 19c, 20b, 21a: 22c, 23b, 24a: 25c, 26a, 27b: 28b, 29c, 30a
31. a-e-i-o-u 32. fairy tales 33. Owl and Pussy-cat 34. Dormouse
35. 3 36. rats 37. Oliver Twist 38. crocodile 39. Jupiter/Zeus 40. 5
41. Christian 42. Gulliver 43. chocolate 44. Gallic 45. Norman Hunter

Sports and Games

1b, 2a, 3c: 4c, 5b, 6a: 7b, 8c, 9a: 10b, 11c, 12a: 13c, 14a, 15b:
16c, 17b, 18a: 19b, 20c, 21a: 22a, 23c, 24b: 25b, 26a, 27c: 28b, 29c, 30a
31. swimming 32. 24 33. golf 34. cycling 35. England v. Australia cricket XIs. 36. 26 37. an unplayable serve 38. 50 39. Roger Bannister
40. Thames 41. wrestling 42. 5 43. free kick at goal 44. boxing
45. steer

Medley 4

1c, 2a, 3b: 4c, 5a, 6b: 7b, 8a, 9c: 10c, 11a, 12b: 13b, 14a, 15c:
16c, 17b, 18a: 19a, 20b, 21c: 22c, 23a, 24b: 25c, 26b, 27a: 28b, 29c, 30a
31. yellow 32. ten 33. copper 34. Good Friday 35. 6 36. May
37. dog 38. swan 39. Pisa, Italy 40. satellite 41. Nyerere
42. Ramadan 43. dollar 44. Pyrenees 45. every four years

Travel

1b, 2c, 3a: 4c, 5b, 6a: 7b, 8c, 9a: 10a, 11b, 12c: 13c, 14a, 15b:
16a, 17c, 18b: 19b, 20c, 21a: 22c, 23b, 24a: 25b, 26c, 27a: 28b, 29c, 30a
31. petrol 32. coal 33. Comet 34. supersonic aircraft 35. supports for railway lines 36. to carry out maintenance 37. Israel 38. on the moon
39. Dover/Calais 40. Switzerland/Italy 41. Cowley, Oxford
42. omnibus 43. 50 miles 44. yellow 45. Australia

Geography

1c, 2a, 3b: 4b, 5a, 6c: 7b, 8c, 9a: 10b, 11c, 12a: 13c, 14a, 15b:
16c, 17b, 18a: 19b, 20c, 21a: 22a, 23c, 24b: 25c, 26a, 27b: 28b, 29a, 30c
31. Mount Everest 32. Brazil 33. Atlantic Ocean 34. Mexico
35. the salt in the sea kills living things 36. Ireland 37. New Zealand
38. Nile 39. Ganges 40. New South Wales 41. Isle of Man
42. Australia 43. Honshu 44. desert 45. a town

Nature
1b, 2c, 3a: 4a, 5b, 6c: 7b, 8c, 9a: 10c, 11b, 12a: 13c, 14b, 15a:
16b, 17a, 18c: 19a, 20c, 21b: 22c, 23a, 24b: 25a, 26c, 27b: 28c, 29b, 30a
31. in a pouch 32. spider 33. in its hump 34. elephant 35. cuckoo
36. giraffe 37. ostrich 38. cheetah 39. kiwi 40. humming bird
41. dandelion 42. cricket 43. brush 44. owl 45. chameleon

Rating Chart

Age	fair	good	excellent
seven	5 – 10	11 – 15	16 +
eight	5 – 10	11 – 17	18 +
nine	10 – 15	16 – 20	21 +
ten	10 – 15	16 – 25	26 +
eleven +	10 – 15	16 – 30	31 +

Questions score 1 point for each correct answer.
Time Tests score 2 points for each correct answer.